Dedications!

Kathy Passage, my mom and Number One Fan...I am always YOUR Number One Fan and appreciate your help on this second book even more. You always remember what to pack for concerts, and you drive me around for special concerts, even when you are tired and it is bad traffic.

Ray Passage, I thank you for your continued encouragement of my music and writing my books. So glad you could come to the Netherlands with me.

Elki and Gordon, our Norwegian elkhound pups—your ears work just like mine and you are never fooled by the digital sirens.

Barbara Gresham Hammerman, president of United by Music North America, and Amanda Gresham, producing artistic director of United by Music in North America - you guys have been so generous with your time and efforts on not only my behalf, but for lots of differently-abled artists as well. www.ubmna.org

United by Music co-founders Joris van Wijngaarden and Candye Kane who put their heads together and imagined a musical extravaganza that would promote blues music, brighten hearts, create cooperation, and blur the lines between who has a disability and who does not. In 2006 their concept became a reality: United by Music. www.unitedbymusic.eu

Dr. Dean Stenehjem, Supt. WSSB, Retired - the encouragement you offered me when I began to write songs like "Bad Behavior Blues" has stayed with me all these years. Thank you so much for your continued support of all my musical endeavors.

NB 11/2022
and Kathy (Mom)

www.mascotbooks.com

Bad Behavior Blues

For more information, please contact:
Mascot Books
620 Herndon Parkway, Suite 320
Herndon, VA 20170
info@mascotbooks.com

Library of Congress Control Number: 2018901575

CPSIA Code: PRT0818A
ISBN-13: 978-1-68401-507-8

Printed in the United States

I've got the Bad Behavior Blues

By Nick Baker, as told to his mom and number one fan, Kathy Passage

Illustrations by Tia Ray

Hi! My name's Nick Baker. I have autism and I am totally blind. Sometimes it's difficult for me to interact with others. I cannot see facial expressions or actions that do not involve physical contact with my body.

My autism makes it hard to understand when people joke around too. I have to rely on what I hear, smell, or feel instead. Sometimes I get frustrated...you would too!

When I get flustered and upset here's what I do to feel better: I use my words. I write songs. Writing lyrics (the words to a song) helps me express my feelings. I create melodies on my keyboard, sing the words into my microphone, mix it all up on my computer, and out comes a song!

"Bad Behavior Blues" was the very first song I wrote. It talks about all the trouble I caused when I rode on the bus back in my school days and learned that words hurt just as much as hitting someone. I've ridden a few other buses during my early school days too, and even later on when I got older and traveled the world. I'm going to tell you about what I learned on those trips too.

The first time I got into trouble on a bus happened when I was in grade school. The special school I attended was too far to walk to, so every morning I rode a big yellow school bus there instead.

There were two ladies on the bus: Mrs. Jones was the driver and Mrs. Ramirez was the helper.

Mrs. Ramirez made sure I was safe as I climbed up all the steps, and she helped me find a seat. When we arrived at the school, she made sure I found the stairs with my cane and held on to the handle when I got off the bus.

It was a very long ride to my school. I sang songs to entertain myself and made lots of noises. I could make bird noises and animal noises, but I especially liked making sounds like cars, trucks, and motorcycles. But my favorite sounds of all were siren sounds. Did you know that there are two kinds of sirens?

Modern vehicles like ambulances use digital devices. Most police cars do too. But fire trucks are special. They have a mechanical type of siren. That means there are parts inside that turn around to make the noises that come out. I can tell the difference between the sirens and so can our dogs, Elki and Gordon.

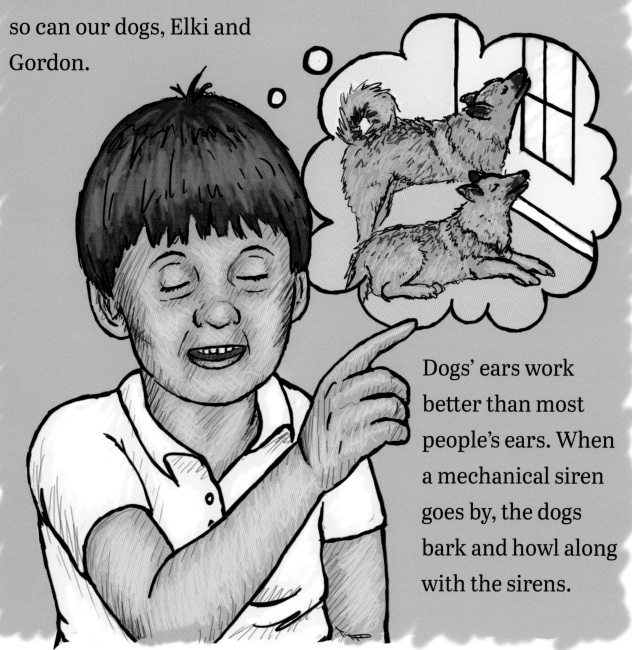

Dogs' ears work better than most people's ears. When a mechanical siren goes by, the dogs bark and howl along with the sirens.

One day while I was riding the bus to school, I heard a fire truck in the distance. My mom always told me that cars have to pull over to the side to allow the big red engine and its crew to pass by safely, and that's just what our bus driver did. The siren got louder as the truck got closer, and then it faded away as the truck moved farther away. Before long, I felt the bus's engine vibrate as it started back on the road

It was a fun little stop, so I thought about other emergency noises. I remembered other ambulance and police car sirens. Pretty soon, siren sounds came out of my mouth, and I felt the bus slow down and bump off to the side of the road again. Then I heard Mrs. Jones say, "I checked the big mirror on the outside of the bus, but I don't see flashing lights or a fire engine."

Mrs. Ramirez said, "I don't see any ambulances. No police cars either."

I heard Mrs. Jones say to her helper, "Take a look back there at Nick Baker. That's where the siren's coming from!"

"Nick Baker!" shouted Mrs. Ramirez. She did not sound happy. I was confused. Most folks liked it when I imitated sounds, but she didn't say "Good job, Nick!" like my teachers or my mom and dad say.

When I got home from school that day, Mrs. Ramirez talked to my mom. "Your son played a trick on us," she said, and then she explained everything. "I even pulled over!"

I did not mean to trick the nice ladies on my bus. Mom apologized and told me a new rule: no more making siren sounds on the school bus. Later that night, I heard my mom tell my dad that she had to put her hand in front of her face to hide a smile when she heard the whole story.

When I got older, I attended the Washington State School for the Blind. It was a residential school where we stayed on campus during the week and learned lots of skills to help us be more independent, like sorting dishes, doing laundry, and keeping our rooms clean.

Every Sunday evening, a charter bus picked me up from my house to take me to school for the week. On Friday afternoons, it dropped me back off at my house. It was a long ride, so the bus helpers would play movies for us. But not everyone had vision, so sometimes kids had other ways of entertaining themselves. It was on this bus that my next adventure happened.

There was a kid named Devon who usually sat in front of me on the bus. Devon's parents always gave him stories on cassette tapes to listen to. Sometimes, when he had trouble playing them, he'd fuss really loudly until they worked.

When that happened, I always listened to understand what was wrong and tried to help him quickly so he'd be quiet. One time, I helped him when the tape player's button was stuck in the off position. I didn't like listening to his whiny voice.

One Sunday, Devon started to fuss and whine. I tried to help him fix his tape, but this time I couldn't make his story play. The bus monitors were busy getting other kids on the bus and into their seats, so they couldn't help either. I was getting frustrated, and Devon was getting louder. Before long, I lost my temper.

Then there was pounding at the windows and more shouting. It was Devon's parents. Mom told me that most parents wait outside the bus to wave to their kids even though we can't see them. I thought that was funny usually, but this time I was glad because one of the bus helpers finally saw them and came down the aisle to help out.

I think they were scared I was going to hurt Devon, but I just wanted him to stop yelling.
It turned out that Devon's parents had forgotten to put a tape in the player. Luckily, they had the tape with them, and as soon as we got it in and hit play, Devon was quiet.

Now I need to tell you the whole story about the bus adventure that inspired my song "Bad Behavior Blues." I was riding the charter bus on my way to WSSB for another week of school. One of my housemates, Rickie, was sitting in front of me. He's blind and has autism just like me. But he was also very different from me. Rickie could not talk. His words came out as sounds that hardly anyone could understand. And since I couldn't see his face, I never knew if he was happy or unhappy.

Stop it Rickie!

That Sunday night, Rickie squawked. He rocked back and forth and bashed his body hard against the bus seat. *Bam, bam.* I could feel the seat jerk just a few inches away from my face. "Rickie, cut it out!" I cried.

He didn't stop. It felt like he was going to break the seat. "Knock it off!" I shouted louder. I banged on the back of his seat. I couldn't bear it, and I couldn't ignore him, so I called him a bad name. I called him a lot of bad names, but even then, he didn't stop.

When one of the bus monitors came to see what was happening, they scolded me. They said what I had done was really bad. When I got to my cottage that night, my house parent came in and took away my radio as punishment for what I had done.

A police officer came to talk with me the next day. "If you were a grown up," he said, "the screaming and mean words you said could have led to an arrest and even time in jail. Verbal attacks are just as bad as actually hitting someone."

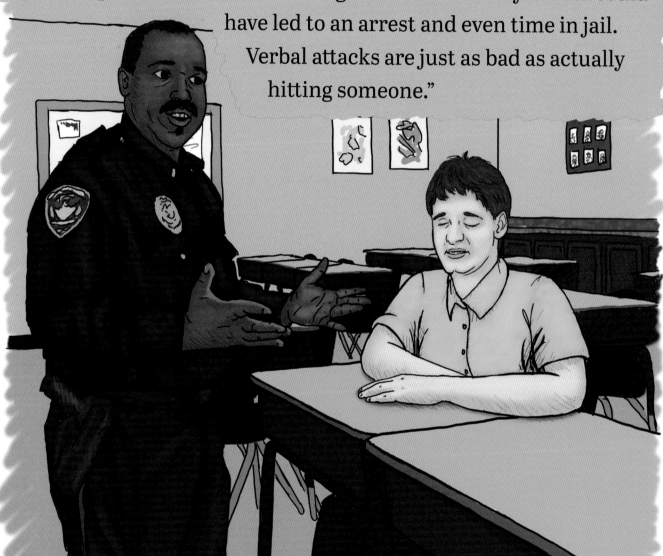

So, the next morning, I made my way to the kitchen to get my breakfast. After I ate, I found Rickie and told him how sorry I was for yelling at him and saying those rude things.

I learned that people like Rickie, who have physical and vocal problems, can't always control their bodies. They just can't help themselves, which means I need to be compassionate and have patience toward others and hope they will respect me right back. *'Cause when you do the wrong thing, man, you're gonna get a case of the Bad Behavior Blues.*

The last bus ride I want to tell you about is the one I went on in the Netherlands with a special group called United by Music North America.

It's a group for people like me who are *differently-abled*. What does that mean? It means musically talented folks who might be blind or have autism, like me, or are in wheelchairs, or have other types of challenges that prevent them from booking their own gigs.

Instead, United by Music North America arranges the details of the concerts for us, so we can go and do what we do best—sing and play our instruments!

But before we get up on a stage, we practice and practice. Professional musicians, called mentors, volunteer to help all of us artists perfect our skills. We have lots of rehearsals to build confidence and polish our act. Soon we are able to perform up on a big stage in front of lots of people.

Next, a very special event happened. I was one of seven artists from our United by Music North America group to travel to the Netherlands. We joined with the members of the United by Music formed in Europe.

The trip was so exciting. My mom and my dad both came. Our dogs had to stay home, which made me a little sad, but I knew I would have plenty to tell them when I got back.

We all flew on a big jet plane over the ocean from Seattle, Washington, to Amsterdam, a city in the Netherlands. It was a long flight too, almost nine hours. I tried to sleep, but I was too excited. I couldn't wait to ride on a bus in a foreign country.

When we arrived, we took a picture of our whole group. We all lined up in front of a huge sculpture at the airport. The letters spelled out Amsterdam!

We rehearsed a lot in the days leading up to the performance. I met lots of new friends, and we all had fun singing together.

When we were ready, we rode special charter buses to the big concert hall. Each bus was driven by one of the United by Music volunteers from the Netherlands, and we all got aboard in our special outfits.

On the way to the concert hall, I heard lots of different sounds. There were new sirens, and I also learned lots of new words from our Dutch bus drivers.

The concert was awesome! Lots of people in the audience wanted to hear us sing. They clapped loudly for each of our songs, and we couldn't wait to come back the next night to sing again.

And guess what song our United by Music group from North America sang?

"Bad Behavior Blues"!

Bad Behavior Blues

Well I've got a real interesting story, a story that is really true.

It has something to do with something I said that was really rude.

Oh baby baby, tell me what am I gonna do. I've been facing a lot of troubles,

I've got the bad behavior blues.

I was riding the charter bus one early Sunday night.

I called my pal Rickie something bad, now baby that just ain't right.

Oh momma, momma someday I'm gonna pay my dues.

I've been facing a lot of troubles; I've got the bad behavior blues.

Well all my teachers told me and so did my mom,

That I would get arrested for the thing that I had done.

It can happen to me, and it can happen to you too.

We all will be prosecuted for the bad things that we do

And that ain't nothing but the cold hard truth kids.

Well I woke up Monday morning and I saw my best pal Rickie.

I told him how sorry I was for saying the things I said that day.

Oh Lord have mercy. You know I'd never say those things to you.

I've been facing a lot of troubles; I've got the bad behavior blues.

Well I've learned my lesson. I've paid my dues.

Oh won't somebody please come help me melt away these blues.

I've been facing a lot of troubles, I've got the bad, I've got the bad,

I've got the bad behavior blues.

If you can't say nothing nice, don't dare say nothing at all!

About the author
Nicholas Alexander Baker

Nick loves music and it is his way of expressing his joys and sorrows in this world. Being born totally blind and later in early adulthood being diagnosed with Autism, he experienced many challenges in his life. Singing and playing music, especially his own original songs, is a healing force in his life.

Nick started writing original music in 2000. Many of his songs have a story behind them, like the book's title, *Bad Behavior Blues.*

In 2008, Nick graduated with honors from Shoreline Community College with an AA degree in Music Performance.

Nick works in his home studio to write, record, engineer, and produce much of his music. Although totally blind, he uses technologies that allow him to work independently. He earns much of his living by performing at assisted living facilities, local restaurants, wineries, and club venues.

Another passion of his is creating jingles for radio and advertising. He recently established his own internet radio show, Nick's Musical Memories: http://www.986themix.com

Nick lives with his mom and stepfather, Kathy and Raymond Passage, and two fluffy Norwegian elkhound pups in Edmonds, Washington, where he participates in community service work at the local senior center. He also visits schools and shares his music and his first book, *"Turtle"*, with students.

To hear Nick's music please visit his website www.nickbakermusic.com.